EXPLORING

CROSVILLE

COUNTRY

· A PAST AND PRESENT COMPANION ·

Aberystwyth—Dolgellau
via Tre'rddol Machynlleth, Corris and Minffordd

Crosville S13, S14, S52

Monday to Saturday	⊕ S1S13	● S13	▲ S13	—	S13	S14	S14	S13	NS S14	S S14	S14	S14	S14	S13	* S13	S13	S13	S14	S13	S S52	S S13
Aberystwyth *Railway Station* ⇌	—	0755	—	0845	—	0920	1150	—	1230	1335	1335	1430	1540	—	1625	1715	1740	1830	—	2030	2230
Waun Fawr *Crossroads*	—	0803	—	0853	—	0928	1158	—	1238	1343	1343	1438	1548	—	1633	1723	1748	1838	—	2038	2238
Waun Fawr *Village*	—	—	—	—	—	0930	1200	—	1240	1345	1345	1440	1550	—	—	—	—	1840	—	2040	—
Commins Coch *Estate*	—	—	—	—	—	0934	1204	—	1244	1349	1349	1444	1554	—	—	—	1844	—	2044	—	
Bow Street *Post Office*	—	0810	—	0900	—	0937	1207	—	1247	1352	1352	—	1557	—	1640	1730	1755	1847	—	2047	2245
Rhydypennau *Fork Roads*	—	0814	—	0904	—	0941	1211	—	1251	1356	1356	—	1601	—	1644	1734	1759	1851	—	2051	2249
Talybont *Square*	—	0818	—	0908	—	0945	1215	—	1254	1359	1359	—	1604	—	1648	1738	1803	1855	—	2055	2253
Tre'rddol *Wildfowler Hotel*	—	—	—	0914	—	0951	1221	—	1300	1405	1405	—	1610	—	1654	1744	1809	1901	—	2101	2259
Eglwysfach *Post Office*	—	—	—	—	—	1000	1230	—	—	1414	1414	—	—	—	1703	—	1818	1910	—	2110	2308
Glandyfi *Station* ⇌	—	—	—	—	—	1002	1232	—	—	1416	1416	—	—	—	1705	—	1820	1912	—	2112	2310
Derwenlas *Black Lion*	—	—	—	—	—	1009	1239	—	—	1423	1423	—	—	—	1712	—	1827	1919	—	2119	2314
Machynlleth *Clock arr.*	—	—	—	—	—	1012	1242	—	—	1426	1426	—	—	—	1715	—	1830	1922	—	2122	2318
Machynlleth *Clock dep.*	—	—	—	—	0924	1012	—	1304	—	1426	1426	—	—	1536	1717	—	—	—	2040	—	—
Machynlleth *Station Approach* ⇌	—	0645	0800	—	0926	1014	—	1306	—	1428	1446	—	—	1538	1719	—	—	—	2042	—	—
Pantperthog *School*	0651	—	0806	—	0932	1020	—	1312	—	1434	1452	—	—	1544	1725	—	—	—	2048	—	—
Esgairgeiliog	0654	—	0809	—	0935	1023	—	1315	—	1437	1455	—	—	1547	1728	—	—	—	2057	—	—
Corris *Post Office*	0659	—	0814	—	0940	—	—	1320	—	—	—	—	—	1552	1733	—	—	—	2102	—	—
Aberllefenni *Post Office*	0704	—	0820	—	0946	—	—	1326	—	—	—	—	—	1558	1739	—	—	—	2108	—	—
Minffordd	—	—	—	—	—	1033	—	—	—	1447	1505	—	—	—	1800	—	—	—	—	—	—
Cross Foxes *Inn*	—	—	—	—	—	1043	—	—	—	1457	1515	—	—	—	1810	—	—	—	—	—	—
Dolgellau *Eldon Square*	—	—	—	—	—	1054	—	—	—	1508	1524	—	—	—	1821	—	—	—	—	—	—

Code:
⇌—Railway Station nearby. ●—Monday to Friday during school terms only. S—Saturdays only
NS—Not Saturdays. ⊕—Monday to Friday, Schooldays only ▲—Via Penglais Comprehensive School
NO SUNDAY SERVICE.

S13.BU

August 1983

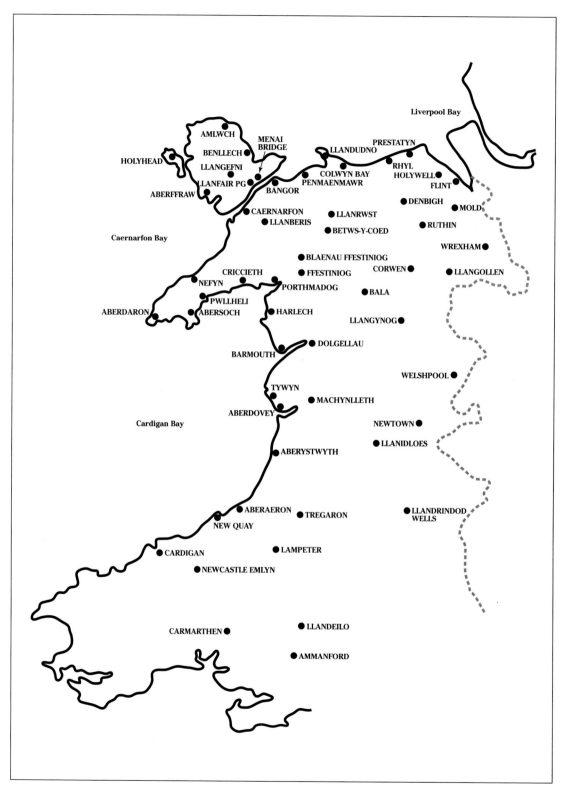

Sketch map showing places in Wales served by Crosville, not all of which are featured in the book.

EXPLORING

CROSVILLE

COUNTRY

· A PAST AND PRESENT COMPANION ·

Part 2: Wales

John Hillmer

·TOWN AND COUNTRY HERITAGE·
from
The NOSTALGIA Collection

First published in 2005

British Library Cataloguing in Publication Data

A catalogue record for this book is available from the British Library.

ISBN 1 85895 249 2

Past & Present Publishing Ltd
The Trundle
Ringstead Road
Great Addington
Kettering
Northants NN14 4BW

Tel/Fax: 01536 330588
email: sales@nostalgiacollection.com
Website: www.nostalgiacollection.com

Printed and bound in Great Britain

A Past & Present book
from
The **NOSTALGIA** *Collection*

Acknowledgements

My thanks go the following who have been generous with their time and/or their photographs: Graham Ashworth, John Baker, John Banks, Ivor Bufton, Alistair Douglas, John Fozard, David Harvey, Chris Heaps, Neville Knight, Kevin Lane, Chris Lodington, Keith Mason, Tony Moyes for his constant support and patience in answering queries, Richard Paramor, Duncan Roberts, Jim Roberts, Gwyn Taylor-Williams, Peter Thompson, Barry Ware, Bryan Wilson, Andrew Woodvine, Barry Wynne, John Young for all his help in identifying non-Crosville buses, and Paul Shannon for the map. I am particularly grateful to John Robinson, for also reading the manuscript and making many helpful suggestions, although I hasten to add that the responsibility for the captions is totally mine and for any errors that may remain, to my wife Geraldine for her expertise in digital scanning and printing, and Will Adams at Silver Link for his advice. Thanks also to the staff at Conwy Library, St Andrews University, for permission to use a Valentines photograph of Caernarfon, and finally to Steve Parry of King's School, Chester, for the translation of the Introduction.

Contents

Bibliography

Anderson, R. C. *History of Crosville* (David & Charles)

Banks, John *Crosville – the Prestige Series* (Venture Publications)

Carroll, John and Roberts, Duncan *Crosville Motor Services, Part 1 The first 40 years* (Venture Publications)

Crosland-Taylor, W. J. *State Owned Without Tears* (Transport Publishing Co Ltd)
    The Sowing and the Harvest (Transport Publishing Co Ltd)

Maund, T. B., FCIT *Crosville on Merseyside* (Transport Publishing Co Ltd)

Maund, T. B., FCIT and Boumphrey, M. *The Wirral Country Bus* (Wirral)

Potter, Bill and Donati, David *2004 Arriva Bus Handbook* (British Bus Publishing Ltd)

Roberts, Duncan *Crosville Motor Services, Part 2 1945-1990* (NBC Books)
    Crosville Motor Services, Part 3 The Successors 1986-2001 (NBC Books)

Robinson, J. P. *Crosville – The Final Harvest* (article in *Buses Extra* 74 (Dec 91/Jan 92), Ian Allan Publishing)

Anyone interested in the Crosville Enthusiasts' Club (1967) should contact John Baker, Secretary, at Park View, 13 Wepre Lane, Connah's Quay, Flintshire CH5 4JR, email Johnbaker_007@hotmail.com.
The Club has its own web site at www.crosville-ec.org.uk

Above TYCOCH: A typical scene in rural Wales, as Bristol RE ERL 527 (PTF 715L), new to Ribble, approaches the A487 at Tycoch, just south of Bow Street, operating the 5.05pm (S10 Route) from the Welsh Breeding Station at Aberystwyth. *A. Moyes*

Gwasanaethau newydd o amgylch Llandudno yn dechrau 16 Tachwedd 1980

New bus services around Llandudno Starting 16th November 1980

L1, M1, M2, M5, M10, M11, M13, M16, M18, M19, M20, M25

CROSVILLE ≫
a NATIONAL bus company

Bilingual cover to Welsh service leaflet.

Left The bilingual cover of a Crosville Welsh service leaflet.

Introduction

Crosville Motor Services was much loved and few bus companies have been so well documented. It speaks for itself that the Crosville Enthusiasts' Club continues long after the company ceased to exist. Founded only a few miles from the Welsh border in Chester, it did not take Crosville long to start running buses in the Principality. Then, by pioneering new territory, acquisition of smaller companies and having parts of other companies such as Western Welsh added, it gradually built up an operating area throughout North, Mid and well into South Wales. The name is still remembered by passengers, and it is said that in Dolgellau people still talk of 'Taking the Crosville'! The point was further driven home by Richard Paramor who, while recently waiting for an X94 Arriva Commander for the short ride to Dolgellau, was told by an elderly lady waiting with him, 'Oh, I do like these new Crosville buses!' While travelling to obtain the 'present' photographs and asking people to pinpoint a particular place in a town for me, several times, when I told them the reason, they replied, 'Oh, my Dad used to work for Crosville.' My own introduction came in the early 1950s when I was a National Serviceman at RAF Hawarden.

The bodywork of all the Crosville buses described in the captions is Eastern Coach Works (ECW) unless otherwise stated, apart from the integral Leyland National, which is simply described as such. I hope the book will give as much pleasure to readers as it has to me in its preparation.

John Hillmer
Wilmslow, Cheshire

Rhagymadrodd

Roedd gwasanaeth moduro Crosville yn boblogaidd tu hwnt a phrin iawn yw'r cwmniau bysiau sydd wedi eu dogfennu cystal. Flynyddoedd ar ôl i'r cwmni ddarfod, gwelir fod llwyddiant clwb brwdfrydig Crosville yn parhau. Sylfaenwyd y cwmni ychydig o filltiroedd o'r ffin â Chymru, ac yn fuan lledaenodd Cwmni Crosville dros yr ardal. Gydag arloesi tiriogaeth newydd, a chaffaeliad cwmniau bychain ac ennill rhannau gan eraill megis y Western Welsh, yn raddol fe dyfodd yr ardal weithredol drwy'r Gogledd, y Canolbarth ac yn ddwfn i Dde-Orllewin Cymru. Mae teithwyr yn dal i gofio'r enw, ac yn ôl y son, mae trigolion Dolgellau yn parhau i ddweud 'Cymryd y Crosville'! Pwysleisiwyd y pwynt ymhellach gan wraig hyn a oedd yn ddisgwyl bws Commander newydd gwasanaeth X94 Arriva Cymru gyda Richard Paramor ar gyfer siwrnai fer i Ddolgellau. Dywedodd "O, dwi yn hoffi'r bysiau Crosville newydd 'ma." Tra'n ymchwilio am luniau o'r presennol gofynnais wrth bobl i fanylu ar lefydd penodol yn y dref i mi. Pan ddywedais wrthynt y rheswm, yn aml cefais yr ymateb, 'O, roedd fy nhad yn arfer gweithio i Crosville.' Daeth fy nghyflwyniad personol yn yr 1950au cynnar pan oeddwn yn Wasanaethwr Cenedlaethol wedi fy lleoli gyda'r Awyrlu Frenhinol yn Mhenarlâg. Gobeithiaf y bydd y llyfr hwn yn rhoi cymaint o bleser i'r darllenwyr ac y gwnaeth i mi wrth ei baratoi.

The development of Crosville territory in Wales

Apart from running services to the Ministry of Munitions factory at Queensferry during the First World War, services started in Mold and Flint in 1919, including Mold to Ruthin via Loggerheads, followed three years later by Llanrwst to Rhyl and Llanrwst to Ruthin. Also in 1922 the purchase of Robert's Blue Motors of Llanrwst brought the route between Betws-y-Coed and Abergele. The year after, the first Express service commenced between New Ferry and Mold, which in 1925 was extended to Loggerheads, where Crosville established a popular leisure site.

Services started in Aberystwyth and Llandrindod Wells in 1924, as did those in Blaenau Ffestiniog, the first route being from Porthmadog. Agreement with the Great Western Railway, and later Western Welsh, took Crosville buses to New Quay, Aberaeron and Cardigan. A small business was acquired in Caernarfon in 1925.

A daily summer service commenced between Liverpool and Loggerheads in 1926, running via Chester and Mold. Express services started from Wirral to Prestatyn and Rhyl, later extended to Llandudno.

By 1929 Crosville was operating on the north coast of Wales, through Rhyl to Bangor, with the area around Holywell already served from the Chester and Mold directions. Another small business was purchased in Caernarfon and new routes were developed alongside those already in existence. The same method of expansion had been applied in Central Wales, down the Cambrian coast.

Late in 1929 Holyhead Motors (Mona Maroon) was added, and 1930 saw an Express service start between Birkenhead and Holywell, but both this and the Woodside to Loggerheads/Denbigh services eventually became stage carriage routes. In 1930 services commenced to Bangor via Holywell, St Asaph, Colwyn and Conway, and a similar one started to Bangor via Corwen and Betws-y-Coed. Also in 1930 Crosville purchased Brookes Bros in Rhyl, North Wales Silver Motors of Llandudno, and W. Edwards of Denbigh.

In 1933 Western Transport Co Ltd of Wrexham was purchased and expansion continued. During the Second World War large demands were made of the company to service munitions factories, and there were many cut-backs on rural routes. A late expansion came in 1972 when the Western Welsh depots and operations at Newcastle Emlyn and New Quay were added to the Crosville territory, which would take its vehicles as far as Carmarthen, and shortly afterwards South Wales Transport transferred its Aberystwyth-Ammanford service to Crosville, together with the outstation at Lampeter, but by then the beginning of the end was in sight. Although no major territorial retrenchment took place until deregulation in 1986, there had been periodic rural cut-backs in the post-1945 era.

Following deregulation, when the Government declared that Crosville was too large, the company was split into two; this saw the start of Crosville Wales, which included Oswestry. The headquarters was established at Llandudno Junction depot and this was followed by a management buy-out at the end of 1987, but in early 1989 the company was purchased by National Express Holdings, which in turn sold out in 1991 to a consortium led by Drawlane. The following year Oswestry depot and the outstation at Abermule were transferred within the Drawlane Group to Midland Red North. All operations were now branded 'Arriva serving Wales/Gwasanaethu Cymru', and today Arriva Cymru is managed under Arriva North West & Wales. Undoubtedly this is by far the largest operator in Crosville's territory in the Principality, working from main depots at Aberystwyth, Bangor, Hawarden, Llandudno Junction, Rhyl and Wrexham, with a number of outstations.

North East Wales

CORWEN DEPOT: London Road depot was opened in 1934, and had an allocation of eight buses in 1947, ten in 1956, 14 in 1965 and 13 in 1970. Photographed in the 1980s, Leyland National SNL 599 (JTU 599T), which was new in 1979, can be seen inside the garage.

The depot remained open after being transferred to Crosville Cymru, before closure came on 1 April 1999, when the premises were sold. The building was adapted for use by the car and van sales firm that now occupies the site, as seen in the 'present' photo taken on 15 February 2005. *Both JCH*

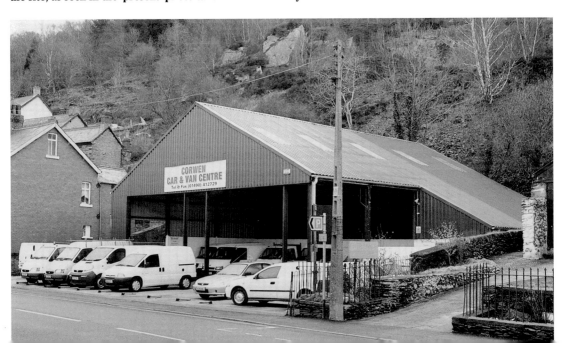

JOHNSTOWN DEPOT: The town is situated a few miles south of Wrexham, and Crosville commenced using Maelor Road depot (an old tram depot) in 1933 following the purchase of Western Transport. The trams were originally horse-drawn, operating from 1876 to 1901, followed by an electric system from 1903 until 1927. The garage's allocation of buses was 19 in 1947, 20 in 1956 and 1965, then down to 17 in 1970, closing two years later in 1972. Crosville's first Bristol SC4LK, SC1 (334 CFM), new in 1957, stands outside the depot where the tramlines can still be seen. To the right of the bus is a board advertising a tour to Rhyl.

Remarkably the building has survived intact, as seen in the photograph of 3 February 2005. Even now it remains possible to see where the tram tracks led into the depot. *John Robinson Collection/JCH*

LLANGOLLEN is the home of the annual International Eisteddfod, and is an attractive town with the River Dee in the centre. The stone bridge is one of the 'Seven Wonders of Wales' and is reputed to be the first crossing of the river. On the northern bank is the station of the preserved Llangollen Railway, which runs to Carrog, with an extension planned to Corwen. The 'past' picture shows a very busy scene with Park Royal-bodied Leyland TD7 M102 (BFN 933) working to Oswestry via Chirk on Service 350. This vehicle was new to Crosville in 1940, having been diverted from East Kent, one of ten buses.

At first glance, placing the two views together is not easy. Photographed again on 3 February 2005, the spire has gone from the church in the background beyond the garage and the body of the church is now a small supermarket. The garage in front of it is the home of Bryn Melyn Motor Services. On the left is the short approach road to the railway station. *John Robinson Collection/JCH*

RUABON is a few miles south of Wrexham, at the 'Gateway' of the Vale of Llangollen. In the 'past' photo, from the late 1950s, Bristol KSW MW 451 (OFM 609) is working on Service D2 to Oswestry with the handsome Parish Church of St Mary's on the left.

On 3 February 2005 it can be seen that there has been a lot of tree growth, partly obscuring the view of the church, which is a 'shared church' between the Church of Wales and the Church of Rome. Bryn Melyn Leyland Lynx UIL 4706 is en route to Llangollen working Service X5 from Wrexham. *John Fozard/JCH*

WREXHAM/WRECSAM is a border town that featured prominently during the Industrial Revolution of the 19th century, with steel-manufacturing at Brymbo, coal-mining and the production of bricks and tiles included among the output. As heavy industry declined the town encouraged new modern ones and has grown considerably, now being a Unitary Authority in its own right, with a first-class shopping centre and a Monday market that is said to be the largest in North Wales. This busy scene shows Bristol LL SLB 289 (NFM 45) loading passengers on Route E3 to Garden Village in June 1969.

On 3 February 2005, with the new bus station concourse behind the photographer, the buildings on the far side of the buses are much the same. To the right is D. Jones & Son's Optare Solo M920 (BU53 DJS) and to the left are two Mercedes-Benz vehicles of G. H. A. Coaches.

The third photograph shows the modern bus station on the same day, with ex-Stagecoach Cambus Volvo B6/Marshall L656 MFL, now with Pat's Coaches of Wrexham.
A. Moyes/JCH (2)

WREXHAM: Approaching the bus station on 22 February 1986, in National Express livery (National Travel West), Duple-bodied Leyland Leopard CLL 325 (YTU 325S) is operating on Route B50. This bus returned to Crosville in 1984 and, following the break-up of the company, was transferred to North Western in 1989.

The scene is much the same 19 years later on 3 February 2005, as M & H Coaches' Dennis Dart/UVG R556 UOT arrives at the bus station on Route 158 from Denbigh. *John Robinson/JCH*

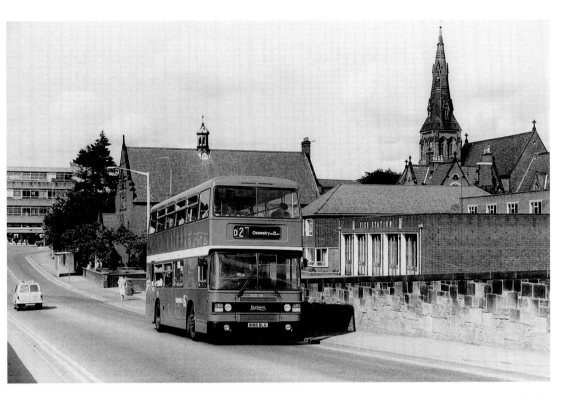

WREXHAM: Leaving the town on 10 June 1985, Leyland Olympian DOG 186 (B186 BLG), on Route D2, heads for Oswestry, having commenced its journey at Chester. When the split came in 1986, this vehicle was transferred to Crosville Wales. Behind the town's Fire Station can be seen St Mary's Cathedral.

There has been little obvious change in the 20 years to 3 February 2005, as Mercedes-Benz/Plaxton Beaver P698 HND, operated by D. Jones & Son, climbs the bridge over the railway. However, considerable changes have taken place nearby, with the cutting back of the rail line to Central and a new station built, together with an impressive shopping area. *John Robinson/JCH*

WREXHAM: In October 1980 Bristol FS DFG 157 (4227 FM) is working on local Route D32 to Prince Charles Road. Behind is the Parish Church of St Giles, considered to be one of the finest medieval churches in Wales. It is believed that a church has been on the site since the 13th century, although the original one was destroyed by fire. The church has close associations with Elihu Yale, after whom Yale University was named, as he was a great benefactor; he was buried in the churchyard and had written the epitaph for his own tombstone before he died.

A great deal of re-development has gone on in the 25 plus years to 3 February 2005, with a Comet store to the left and a Halfords to the right, but the church remains as ever, as does the ornamental chimney from the former Border Brewery, dating only from 1894! One wonders whether planning permission would have been granted today for a brewery next to the church! A Strafford's coach is passing the mini-roundabout. *A. Moyes/JCH*

WREXHAM, MOLD ROAD DEPOT: Built on a 'green field' site and opened in the early 1930s, the depot usually had an allocation of more than 100 buses. On Sunday 11 September 1983 the first picture shows immaculate parking, with Leyland Nationals outside the garage and Bristol VRs inside, then in the second photo we see a perfect line-up of 17 Bristol LHs. The third shot was taken after the split, and shows Bristol MW recovery vehicle G581 (HFM 581D) on 18 April 1989. This was new to Crosville in 1966 as EMG 581, and converted in 1981.

Transferred later to Crosville Cymru, today there is absolutely nothing left of the depot. The site was cleared and a housing estate built, as seen in the fourth picture of 3 February 2005. *JCH (2)/John Robinson/JCH*

North Wales

ABERDARON is almost at the end of the Lleyn peninsula. This tiny resort is popular with holiday-makers with a long history as the point of embarkation for Bardsey Island, used by pilgrims right back to the 14th century and by bird-watchers and day-trippers today. In September 1981 Bristol LH SLL 626 (OCA 626P) negotiates the narrow bridge out of the village as it leaves for Pwllheli working on Route R11.

On the beautiful morning of 24 March 2005, the equivalent is Route 17B operated by Arriva, on this occasion with Dennis Dart/Plaxton Pointer 1130 (N707 GUM). The journey time is 45 minutes to Pwllheli. *Keith Mason/JCH*

ABERSOCH, situated on the south side of the Lleyn peninsula, was once a fishing village and has now developed as a busy holiday destination, particularly for yachting enthusiasts and their families. Daimler Fleetline HDL 917 (XUF 387K) is arriving from Pwllheli working on Route 19 in September 1984. This vehicle was acquired from Southdown Motor Services in 1980.

Just over 20 years later, on 14 March 2005, Arriva Dennis Dart/Plaxton Pointer 1130 (N707 GUM) is on Route 18 to Pwllheli. There have been a few minor changes to the buildings, but the scene is much the same – cars continue to park on the bus stop! *Keith Mason/JCH*

BALA/Y BALA is a small town situated between Llangollen and Dolgellau, close by Bala Lake (Llyn Tegid). It holds an important place in the history of the Nonconformist Church, and in the 18th century it had a thriving woollen industry. On 25 August 1990 Crosville Cymru DAF Optare Delta SDD 702 (F702 ECC) is at the bus stop in the main street on Service 94 running between Barmouth and Wrexham.

The number of services in the winter of 2004/5 was decidedly thin, and we have to be content with a rear view of Arriva DAF/Northern Counties Paladin 1796 (N24 FWU) working to Barmouth on 15 February 2005. *Chris Lodington/JCH*

Below BALA: Looking eastwards on 27 May 1986, Bristol RE SRG 113 (AFM 113G) is arriving in the town on the same Route D94, which normally ran between Wrexham and Bala, although some services worked between Corwen and Bala. *P. J. Thompson*

BANGOR is a University city, close by the Menai Strait, with a Cathedral that has probably been in continuous use longer than any other in the UK – the present building, which was totally restored by Sir George Gilbert Scott, dates back to the 13th century. Visitors often approach from the east and see this view, with the Menai Strait on the right and the city centre on the left; the Victorian pier has been beautifully restored. In this photograph taken in the late 1970s, along Beach Road, Bristol RE SRG 126 (DFM 126H) heads east on a local Service M78 to Maesgeirchen.

The view is now somewhat restricted by tree growth, as seen on 22 February 2005, as Arriva Leyland Lynx 1755 (J655 UHN) climbs the hill showing 'Not in Service'. The bus was allocated to Bangor depot at this time. *Barry Wynne/JCH*

BANGOR, BEACH ROAD DEPOT: Opened in 1931, in 1947 the depot's allocation was 54, down to 42 in 1970. It was subsequently handed over to Crosville Cymru, later to become an Arriva garage with 69 vehicles in 2001, and outstations at Amlwch, Caernarfon, Holyhead and Pwllheli. In this view from the early 1960s, there is a variety of Bristols present, including three MWs, two Lodekkas and two SCs.

On the cold morning of 22 February 2005, outside the garage are Arriva Leyland Lynx 1751 (H34 PAJ) and Volvo Olympian/Northern Counties Palatine 3357 (P94 MKL), awaiting their next turns of duty. The depot building appears to be much the same. *Barry Wynne/JCH*

New Bus Gwynedd-liveried Clipas by the depot on 4 October 1987. *Barry Wynne*

BANGOR: One summer in the 1970s, Bristol RE CRG 161 (EFM 161H), new in 1970, has come down Stryd Fawr, passes the Plaza cinema and is about to take a right turn into Station Road, showing Route N45 on the blind.

Due to foliage growth a repetition of the exact position for the 'present' picture was not possible, but from street level the cinema building appears little changed – now called the Apollo –although there is a new building beyond. Arriva DAF SB200/Wright Commander 2506 (CX54 EPL) is working on Route X32 to Aberystwyth. *Barry Wynne/JCH*

One of the six Leyland Tiger TS8s new in 1939 and numbered KA148-53 (DFM 519-24) stands outside the cinema on 3 July 1952 – note the starting handle. *N. R. Knight*

BARMOUTH/ABERMO (Abermaw or Y Bermo) is a busy holiday resort on the northern side of the Mawddach Estuary, over which it is possible to walk using the ex-Cambrian Railways bridge to Morfa Mawddach. Around 1963, Bristol SC SSG 652 (649 LFM) is seen on Service S34 to Dolgellau as it passes along the busy High Street.

Unfortunately, for the 'present' picture, a wide load got into difficulties and the street was blocked for a period, so photographing a bus proved impossible! There have been a number of changes to the surrounding buildings, as seen on 15 February 2005. *John Fozard/JCH*

BARMOUTH: There was a Crosville presence in the town from 1923 when a depot was opened at the Min-y-Mor Laundry. A new garage was built in the early 1950s, which remained open until 1991, when the lease was surrendered and the building demolished. The allocation of vehicles was four in 1947, eight in 1956 and nine in 1965. At the Marine Parade parking ground and office in about 1963, Bristol SC SSG 653 (650 LFM) waits its next turn of duty on Route S35 to Harlech. On the left is the quite substantial Crosville office and in front of the Mona Café the tender of BR Standard Class 4 4-6-0 No 75027 can be seen; this engine is now preserved on the Bluebell Railway.

Buses no longer park on the sea side of the railway, but looking across the railway tracks, towards the town, Express Motors Mercedes-Benz/Plaxton Beaver S310 DLG is seen awaiting departure time on 15 February 2005. *John Fozard/JCH*

BETWS-Y-COED: This well-known inland resort has been famous since the coming of the railway in Victorian times. Many walkers use it as a centre for exploring the beautiful countryside and visiting the attractions of the Conwy Falls near the Fairy Glen, as well as the Swallow Falls and the many other delights to be enjoyed. On a lovely summer's day in the late 1960s, Bristol MW EMG 582 (HFM 582D) stands outside the railway station, perhaps awaiting the arrival of a train, and showing 'Capel Curig M99' on the blinds.

As popular as ever, there have been developments beyond the railway station and shops, with a new bus turning circle and stand used by several services. On 9 March 2005 Arriva Mercedes-Benz Vario/Plaxton Beaver 325 (R795 DUB) works Route 19 to Llandudno from Llangollen. *David Harvey Collection/JCH*

BLAENAU FFESTINIOG is in the heart of the slate country and at one time was known as the 'Slate Capital of Wales'; one of the old quarries (Llechwedd Slate Cavern) has become a major tourist attraction. The slate waste heaps remain, but there are plans afoot to remove them by rail, as there is an economic use for the material in road building following the introduction of a tax on new quarrying. It was slate that was originally carried by the narrow-gauge steam line to Porthmadog, now one of the popular 'Great Little Railways of Wales'. On 28 August 1985 ex-Ribble Bristol VR DVG 574 (NCK 984K) fills up with passengers wishing to visit the interesting Slate Mines Centre.

On 9 March 2005 John's Coaches Mercedes-Benz/Plaxton Beaver N671 TPF heads for Tan-y-Grisiau working Route 37. There has been quite a lot of change in the main street, as can be seen in the 'present' photograph. *Chris Lodington/JCH*

BLAENAU FFESTINIOG: Bristol LL6B KW 291 (NFM 47) awaits its departure time working to Tan-y-Grisiau and Llanrwst. This vehicle was new in 1952.

On 9 March 2005, Express Motors Dennis Dart/Plaxton S1 EMS has arrived on Route 1 from Caernarfon. *John Robinson Collection/JCH*

BLAENAU FFESTINIOG: The new North Western Road depot was opened in 1964, replacing the original one in the High Street. The allocation in 1947 was 11, in 1956 it was 13, in 1965 nine, and seven in 1970. With the rather forbidding wintry background in February 1981 there are three buses to be seen, a Bristol LH on the left and two dual-purpose Bristol REs together with Sherpa 15cwt van 90A (BMA 942S), new in January 1978. The depot was in use until September 1990, but there had been problems with subsidence and vandalism, so Portakabins were used to replace the permanent buildings and the depot re-opened to house half a dozen buses. Closure came again in September 1995 and the site has subsequently been sold.

Today the area remains in use as a bus garage by John's Coaches, as seen on 9 March 2005. Former Shearings DAF MB200/Plaxton Paramount 3200 ANA 449Y is on the left, and DAF MB230/Plaxton Paramount 3500 JIB 1470 by the building. Although the old garage was demolished there remains a small building at the rear that links the two pictures together. *A. Moyes/ JCH*

At the depot on 20 July 1985 are (from left to right) Leyland National SNL 661 (GMB 661T), ex-Southdown Daimler Fleetline HDL 918 (XUF 398K), which obscures Bristol LH SLL 640 (OCA 640P), then SLL 636 (OCA 636P) and, on extreme right, Bristol RE SRG 182 (EFM 182H). *JCH*

BODELWYDDAN is famed for the 'Marble Church' (in fact the elegant white spire was made from local limestone), which is a well-known landmark to look out for as one approaches the North Wales coast on the A55. Bristol VR DVG 462 (VCA 462W) was new to Crosville in 1980 and is working on Route M5 to Rhyl.

With the up-grading of the A55 to dual carriageway (now to the right of the photographer), the church has been by-passed, as seen in the 'present' photo of 2 March 2005. Arriva Mercedes-Benz Vario/Plaxton Beaver 305 (R805 YJC) picks up passengers travelling east. *Keith Mason/JCH*

Opposite CAERNARFON was the site of a Roman military settlement around AD78, and much later Edward I built a magnificent castle here, one of the chain of fortresses in North Wales. It was here that Prince Charles was invested as Prince of Wales in 1969. This wonderful view, looking down from the castle ramparts on to Castle Square below, dates back to about 1955. Several Crosville vehicles can be seen, including a lightweight Leyland-Beadle integral rebuild and a Bristol K double-decker. Note the line of people waiting for their bus, knowing exactly where it will stop!

Getting on for 40 years later, on 18 June 2004, the square is no longer used for service buses, having been partly pedestrianised, although an occasional coach comes through to reach a parking place. The statue to the memory of Syr Hugh Owen remains, amidst the thriving trees. The Presbyterian Church in Wales (centre) is a good starting point for comparison between 'past' and 'present'. *Valentine Collection, courtesy St Andrews University Library/JCH*

CAERNARFON: In a busy scene during October 1997 at Penllwyn, where there are a number of bus stands, on the left we see ECW-bodied Leyland Olympian DOG 509 (CWR 509Y), which was ex-West Riding Group, on Route 86 to Penygroes and Talysarn, with Northern Counties-bodied Leyland Olympian DOL 103 (A103 OUG), which was also ex-West Riding Group but new to South Yorkshire Road Transport, by Stand A on the Bangor service.

By 18 June 2004 the building on the right has been completed and the street remains the starting point for most services. In the foreground is Silver Star Mercedes-Benz/Plaxton Beaver L775 RWW showing Cae Gwyn on Route 92, a local service. An Arriva single-decker can be seen further back on the right. *A. Moyes/JCH*

CAERNARFON, BANGOR ROAD DEPOT opened in 1932, and in 1937 additional land was purchased adjacent to it. In the photo taken in October 1986 we get a fine view of the buildings, with a variety of buses including a Crosville Bova Futura coach in National Express livery, a Bristol RE, a Duple-bodied Leyland Tiger and a Bristol LH. In 1947 the allocation was 44, but this had been reduced to 25 in 1980. The depot remained in use by Crosville Cymru until sold to Kwik Save for re-development in 1991.

The same scene on 18 June 2004 shows the outcome, a supermarket – only the church of St David & St Helen remains in the background. Express Motors Optare Spectra EM04 ORS heads towards the roundabout; this vehicle is notably one of the last of the type to have been built. *A. Moyes/JCH*

COLWYN BAY/BAE COLWYN is a popular holiday resort with a long and attractive promenade. The Victorian Pier, opened in 1900, was extended from 316 feet to 750 feet, but the Pavilion was to suffer two serious fires. Since 1968 it has changed hands several times, but it is hoped that the current owners will be able to start restoration work. Northern Counties-bodied Leyland Titan TD1 L115 (CK 4222), new to Ribble in 1930 and acquired by Crosville from Bristol Tramways & Carriage Company in 1949, stands in front of the railway station on Route 414 to Llandudno Junction via Mochdre in June 1951.

The Imperial Hotel remains, little changed, as do the buildings along Station Road, as seen on 25 June 2004. No service buses head east along Victoria Avenue in front of the station, so we have to be content with westbound Arriva Mercedes-Benz/Plaxton Beaver 339 (R109 TKD) on a local service. *G H F Atkins © John Banks Collection/JCH*

COLWYN BAY: In the late 1950s Bristol LS EUG 339 (488 AFM), working on Route P3 to Bangor, is near the railway station. The vehicle was fitted for one-man operation from new in 1956.

Considerable alterations to the forecourt of the station have been made and buses do not pass in the same direction. Although the buildings remain much the same, there appears to have been more space around them compared with the 'present' photo of 22 February 2005, as Arriva Mercedes-Benz Vario/Plaxton 332 (R102 TKO) manoeuvres past parked vehicles, heading for Colwyn Heights. *John Fozard/JCH*

COLWYN BAY: How can one resist a photograph such as this, even if there is no direct Crosville connection? However, there is an indirect one, for when the Llandudno & Colwyn Bay Electric Railway came to an end with trams and then with its own fleet of replacement buses, Crosville bought the routes and goodwill. Car No 8 is seen moving down Conway Road; built in 1907, it remained in service until 1936. The tramway lasted until 1956, followed by buses until 1961, when Crosville took over.

The view of the main street has not changed that much, as seen on 22 February 2005, except that Barclays Bank on the corner has had a 'make-over'. There is constant traffic, including Arriva buses – Mercedes Benz Vario/Plaxton Beaver 327 (R797 DUB) approaches on Route 14, for Conwy, but via Llandudno! *Jim Roberts Collection/JCH*

CONWY/ABERCONWY: Until late 1958, when the new road bridge over the estuary from Llandudno Junction to Conwy was opened, there were narrow arches to be negotiated. Dennis EV U47 (JC 46) is just about squeezing through as it enters Conway (as it was then spelled). It is possible that this photograph was taken in the early 1930s before Owens of Llandudno Junction had been purchased by Crosville. To the immediate right of the arch was the Fire Station, nestling by the side of Edward I's castle, considered to be one of Europe's best examples of a medieval fortress.

The arch had to be demolished before the new road could be completed, but on 24 March 2005 it was still possible to see its exact position, as the stonework to the left of the bus can be matched to the 'past' picture. Alpine-operated school bus Leyland Olympian/ECW B155 TRN was new to Ribble and came to Alpine via North Western and Arriva. *G H F Atkins © John Banks Collection/JCH*

CONWY, LANCASTER SQUARE: Nearby is the historic 14th-century Aberconwy House, under the care of the National Trust. Bristol SC SSG 626 (566 JFM), new in 1959, is seen here in 1973 with 'M93 Pant-y-Tan' on the blind.

Thirty-one years later, on a rather misty 5 August 2004, Arriva Mercedes-Benz/Plaxton Beaver 327 (R797 DUB) is on Service 15 to Ysbyty Glan Clwyd via Llandudno. Most of the shops have changed hands, the Square has been semi-pedestrianised (a carefully laid road surface of blocks has replaced tarmac), but sadly even the nearby hills are not visible. *Chris Heaps/JCH*

CONWY, BANGOR ROAD: In 1973 Bristol RE ERG 60 (UFM 60F) squeezes through one of the arches of the town walls as it heads towards Caernarfon on Service L1, the Cymru Coastliner, which ran from Chester via Llandudno and Bangor.

On 5 August 2004 K. M. P. Volvo/Wright Eclipse N777 KMP must have found it an equally tight fit. The bus is on Service 9 to Holyhead via Bangor (subsequently cut back to Llangefni). The marking on the walls has not changed in the 30-odd years, and of course the No Entry signs remain. *Chris Heaps/JCH*

CRICCIETH/CRICIETH is located between Pwllheli and Porthmadog on the busy A497. It has two beaches, divided by a headland dominated by the considerable remains of a Welsh castle, later enhanced by Edward I, with glorious coastal views and a massive round-towered gatehouse. Crosville Cymru open-top Bristol VR DVG 519 (YMB 519W) is employed on Route 3A heading west to Pwllheli in June 1995.

The Porthmadog to Pwllheli service remains as Route 3, but is now shared between Arriva and Caelloi of Pwllheli. On 24 March 2005 Caelloi DAF/Wright CX51 FKO leaves for the latter town. *Keith Mason/JCH*

DENBIGH/DINBYCH is a town with a long history, containing many old buildings and the ruins of a castle. The county town of the shire, one of its famous sons was H. M. Stanley, the rescuer of Dr Livingstone, and another was local bard Twm o'r Nant. On 31 August 1985 Bristol RE ERG 280 (YFM 280L) is seen in the town centre working on Route M76, having arrived from Ruthin.

Nearly 20 years later, on 9 March 2005, Arriva Mercedes-Benz Vario/Plaxton Beaver 302 (R802 YJC) has pulled in from Rhyl working Route 51. *Chris Lodington/JCH*

DENBIGH, LENTEN POOL DEPOT was acquired with the purchase of Brookes' business in 1930. On market days buses from other depots augmented the allocation, which in 1947 stood at 21 buses, in 1956 it was 28, the same number in 1965, and 17 in 1970. The building was altered in 1948 to accommodate double-deckers, and remained open under Crosville Cymru until 1990, when it became redundant, ultimately becoming a Market Hall. In 1949 a Leyland Titan PD1A stands in front of the garage showing St Asaph Route 427A on the lower blind.

The second photo shows that there were subsequently some modifications to the building and a new Crosville name added. Bristol VR DVG 475 (WTU 475W), new in 1981, peeps out, and to the right is a notice stating 'Double deckers are not to turn inside depot', while above is stated the maximum height, 14ft 4in or 4.369m.

After usage as a Market Hall, it has now become 'TJ's Market World', as seen in the third picture dated 9 March 2005. *CMS/JCH (2)*

DOLGELLAU is set in beautiful countryside close to Cader Idris and the Mawddach Estuary. The buildings are mostly of stone, which gives the town its very solid character. Its history dates back to the 12th century, and Owain Glyndwr held his last Parliament of Free Wales here in 1404. In modern times it is well known as an 'Interchange', where buses arrive at the same time from different directions, making Eldon Square a scene of great activity. On 12 July 1997 ex-Colchester Borough Transport Leyland Lynx SLC 39 (G39 YHJ), in Crosville Cymru livery and on Route 94 to Barmouth, has pulled in at the SAFLE BWS to pick up a guitar-carrying passenger.

Eldon Square remains a busy interchange several times a day. In the picture of 15 February 2005, Arriva DAF/Van Hool 5003 (M945 LYR) is employed on Route X32 to Bangor, while behind it is Arriva Leyland Lynx 1755 (J655 UHN) heading in the opposite direction to Aberystwyth. In the winter of 2005 the X32 operated between Aberystwyth and Bangor and the 701 from Porth/Cardiff to Aberystwyth. *Chris Lodington/JCH*

DOLGELLAU: In September 1986 Bristol VR DVL 390 (FTU 390T) is leaving the town across the new bridge heading for Blaenau Ffestiniog employed on Route R35. Cader Idris rises majestically in the background.
    Shooting almost directly into the sun on the bright winter's day of 15 February 2005 creates one or two sunbursts as Celtic Self Drive LDV Convoy minibus P855 JTR approaches the junction. *A. Moyes/JCH*

DWYGYFYLCHI: With the lower slopes of Penmaenmawr mountain in the background, and seen from the iron footbridge that crosses from the Little Chef over the A55 and the railway to the beach, Bristol VR DVG 511 (YMB 511W), in 'Happy Dragon' livery, heads towards Conwy on Route 5 from Caernarfon to Llandudno in the mid-1990s. The bus was new to Crosville in 1981, then transferred to Crosville Cymru in 1986.

A very cold wind is blowing in from the sea on the morning of 2 March 2005 as Alpine Leyland Olympian/ECW TBX 713 (ex-EWX 531W) approaches on a school run. Originally new to West Riding, it moved to Arriva Yorkshire before spending some time with Crosville Cymru (DOG 531). *Ivor Bufton/JCH*

45

DYSERTH is just a few miles inland from Prestatyn, below the slopes of Graig Fawr, and is well known for the nearby waterfall, which drops 80 feet. On 12 August 1965 Bristol FS DFB 138 (4206 FM), new in 1963, is working the Rhyl-Rhuddlan-Prestatyn-Rhyl circular.

Almost 40 years later, on 10 November 2004, the scene has changed very little except that Gwalia Stores is no longer a shop. Arriva Dennis Dart/Plaxton Pointer 831 (X271 RFF) makes the same right turn towards the village, working on Route 36, which operates between Rhyl and Rhuddlan. *A. Moyes/JCH*

GREENFIELD: Along the A548 from Connah's Quay to Prestatyn, Leyland Olympian EOG206 (C206 GTU), with the Welsh Dragon symbol on the side, heads north-west close by the Dee Estuary on 9 May 1986, working on Service L1 to Caernarfon. Behind is the railway bridge that carried the branch line from Holywell Junction to Holywell, which closed in 1954.

The railway bridge remains in situ as a Leyland Tiger of P & O Lloyd of Bagillt, with an East Lancs rebody, is about to turn right on 10 November 2004. *John Robinson/JCH*

GREENFIELD INDUSTRIAL ESTATE: Until the early 1980s Courtaulds had the largest viscose rayon spinning operation in the UK on the Greenfield Business Park site, employing 3,000 people. On 16 July 1975 Bristol RE SRG 101 (XFM 101G) is employed on a Works Service, showing Holway (near Holywell) on the blind. Above the factory roof can be seen the Wirral coastline on the far side of the Dee Estuary.

Today, as we can see in the 'present' photograph dated 10 November 2004, the industrial buildings have been swept away and the area has been re-developed into a modern Industrial Park. Only the brick gateposts have survived. The majority of people working in the various units would appear to use their cars, judging by the number parked, so it is doubtful whether any buses enter the Park these days. *A. Moyes/JCH*

HARLECH lies on the west coast of Wales at the north end of Cardigan Bay between Porthmadog and Barmouth. Another of Edward I's 13th-century medieval castles was built here in a commanding position overlooking the sea on one side and the surrounding countryside on the other. Nonetheless, at the end of the 14th century Owain Glyndwr took the castle, although Harry of Monmouth retook it around 1408. Several hundred years later, on 13 May 1977, Bristol RE ERG 6 (OFM 6E) stands in the Castle Square at the top of the hill employed on Service R38, which operated between Dolgellau and Maentwrog. With the castle on the left, beyond the bus lies a wonderful panoramic view.

On the beautiful sunny day of 15 February 2005, with snow on the tops of the distant mountains, the castle has not changed but no longer do buses reach the area close to the entrance. *Barry Ware/JCH*

HOLYWELL/TREFFYNNON takes its name from the Holy Well of St Winefride, one of the 'Seven Wonders of Wales' and a destination for pilgrims for many years. On 9 May 1986 Leyland National ENL 961 (MLG 961P) is en route to Maes Pennant showing Service A4 on the blind.

Eighteen years later, on 10 November 2004, the view is much the same although the town's by-pass has been modernised. Arriva Dennis Dart/Plaxton Pointer 844 (Y544 UJC) is employed on Route 11 between Rhyl and Chester. *John Robinson/JCH*

LLANBERIS, situated at the foot of Snowdon, is an ideal centre for touring the area. It is also home for two narrow-gauge railways – the Snowdon Mountain Railway and the Llanberis Lake Railway. On 6 August 1960 Bristol SC SSG 649 (646 LFM), new in March of that year, awaits its departure time on Service N76 to Bangor.

A new bus turning point and stand have been built, as seen on 9 March 2005, with the two railway stations close by. Arriva Volvo Olympian/Northern Counties Palatine 3357 (P940 MKL) is working on Route 87 to Bangor. *A. J. Douglas/JCH*

LLANDUDNO is undoubtedly the finest of the North Wales seaside towns – reference to it as the 'Queen of the Welsh Resorts' is well justified. Much is due to the care with which the Mostyn family watched over its development, the even height of the buildings along the promenade being a good example of their stewardship. The town is dominated by the Great Orme, which has its own tramway, while the Victorian pier is the fifth longest in the UK at 2,295 feet. Ex-North Western Park Royal-bodied AEC Renown DAA 501 (VDB 964), employed on Service X3 to Liverpool, passes along the Promenade in September 1972.

Today there are no regular service bus routes along the Promenade other than the Alpine sightseeing tours. On 25 June 2004 open-top ex-Crosville Cymru Park Royal-bodied Leyland Atlantean JPL 105K works the Llandudno & Conwy Tour. *John Banks Collection/JCH*

LLANDUDNO: In August 1931, recently delivered all-Leyland Lion LT2 441 (FM 6420) passes along Mostyn Street. Despite the passage of 73 years, on 5 August 2004 the scene is not so very different. Just beyond the Methodist church of St John's, a new building has been erected and is occupied by Marks & Spencer. The Great Orme forms the backdrop as Arriva Dennis Dart/Plaxton Pointer 7564 (R564 ABA) is seen on Route 5 to Caernarfon. *John Banks Collection/JCH*

LLANDUDNO: Plaxton-bodied Leyland Leopard ELL 314 (RMA 314P), working on Route M5 to Caernarvon, is seen in Mostyn Street in June 1980. The vehicle was delivered new to Crosville in 1976 as CLL 314, but was later downgraded from coach status ('C') to Express ('E').

The same view on 5 August 2004 shows a similar scene with Arriva Mercedes-Benz/Plaxton Beaver 347 (R117 TKO) operating on Route 26, which runs from Llandudno to Tan Lan via Mochdre. *G H F Atkins © John Banks Collection/JCH*

LLANDUDNO: Caught by the camera in June 1933 on Oxford Road, all-Leyland Tiger TS2 177 (FM 5224), new in 1929, is well filled as it heads for Liverpool with a long-distance service.

    Although today Oxford Road is not used by any buses, on the Bank Holiday Monday of 2 May 2005, during the Victorian Transport Extravaganza weekend, preserved Crosville Bristol LL5G KG 150 (LFM 731) was in the right place at the right time! *G H F Atkins © John Banks Collection/JCH*

LLANDUDNO DEPOT at Mostyn Broadway opened in 1931, the third in the town. The allocation in 1947 was 21, and the depot lasted 40 years, when all workings and vehicles were transferred to Llandudno Junction garage. On 11 August 1960 Bristol SC coach CSG 629 (190 KFM) stands outside.

Following closure, the site was re-developed and became a motor showroom and filling station. Beyond, the Grand Theatre (from where BBC broadcasting took place during the Second World War) remains but is now the Broadway Boulevard Discotheque. In our 'present' picture of 25 June 2004, Arriva Dennis Dart/Plaxton Pointer 2353 (V583 DJC), on Route 12 to Rhyl, is seen leaving the town. *A. J. Douglas/JCH*

LLANDUDNO DEPOT: Looking in the other direction, towards the town in July 1970, this photo shows three coaches of different styles parked outside the garage. From right to left, they are Bristol MWs CMG 358 (806 FFM), CMG 482 (2188 FM) and Duple-bodied Bedford CVF 694 (XFM 694G).

On 11 August 2004 all that remains to link the two photographs is the wall on the extreme right of the 'present' picture. Arriva Mercedes-Benz/Plaxton Beaver 346 (R116 TKO) is employed on Service 12 to Rhyl, while a Cumbria Coaches vehicle can be seen inside the filling station. *G H F Atkins © John Banks Collection /JCH*

LLANDUDNO JUNCTION/CYFFORDD LLANDUDNO: Glan-y-Mor Road Depot opened in 1931, with an allocation of 47 in 1947, which rose slightly to 51 in 1980. In this September 1982 photograph, looking down on the front of the depot, five double-deckers are on view, including Bristol VR DVG 506 (YMB 506W) foremost on the right, delivered new in 1981. In 1986 the depot became the headquarters of the Welsh part of the Group.

Twenty-two years later, on the misty morning of 5 August 2004, other than a change of name the depot looks much the same, although there have been some alterations on the forecourt. Parked outside we see Arriva ex-Merseybus Leyland Olympian/Alexander open-topper 3987 (E227 WBG), showing Route 101 on the blind. *John Fozard/JCH*

LLANRWST: The narrow bridge over the River Conwy has been a bottleneck since it was built in 1636! On 19 July 1966 Bristol LL6B SLB 284 (NFM 40) on Route M19 to Llandudno is about to cross the border into Caernarfonshire, and is hoping to have a clear way across – so often vehicles reach this point and see that there is another heading towards them, so have no option but to reverse on to the main road behind. Imagine what it is like when several vehicles are involved! Undoubtedly it was even worse in the days of horse-drawn vehicles.

Apart from the fact that the Victoria Hotel is no longer available for lunch, nothing much has changed by 5 August 2004, getting on for 40 years later. The bus is Arriva-operated Mercedes-Benz/Plaxton Beaver 323 (R793 DUB) on the same Route 19 bound for Llandudno. *A. Moyes/JCH*

LLANRWST DEPOT: The first base was set up at the Victoria Hotel garage in 1923, then Royal Blue opened the present garage at Betws-y-Coed Road in 1929, and Crosville moved in to share the premises. In 1931 it had an allocation of 13 vehicles, but by 1968 it had been reduced to outstation status, half of the premises being let to tyre fitters Jones Bros; it remained as an outstation for Crosville Cymru under Llandudno Junction. In the photo taken on 9 August 1960, Bristol L6A SLA 58 (GFM 867) is seen outside the garage with Corwen on the blind.

Almost exactly 44 years later, on 5 August 2004, Arriva Mercedes-Benz/Plaxton Beaver 323 (R793 DUB) is in a similar position but with Betws-y-Coed Route 19 showing on the blind. The nearer half of the building is used for buses, and it is still an outstation to Llandudno Junction with an allocation of six vehicles. It appears that the building behind the bus in the 'past' picture has been demolished, and we can now see much more of the further one. *A. J. Douglas/JCH*

MENAI BRIDGE: Crossing the Strait on 7 July 1982, Bristol FLF DFG 256 (SFM 256F) nears the mainland operating on School Bus Route M9, having worked to David Hughes School. Telford's famous suspension bridge was opened in 1826 with a weight restriction, but following a heavy gale it was necessary to reconstruct it in steel in place of the original iron. After re-building (without closure to traffic) the restriction was lifted, and the toll ceased on 31 December 1940. The first double-decker crossed the bridge in 1945.

Due to repainting of the bridge, only the southbound carriageway was open on 2 March 2005 – northbound traffic to the island had to use the Britannia Bridge. Arriva Dennis Dart/Plaxton Pointer 815 (T565 JJC) is employed on Route 47 from Llanfair PG to Bangor. *A. Moyes/JCH*

MOLD/YR WYDDGRUG is the county town of Flintshire and also the administrative headquarters. Busy with markets on two days a week and home of the highly acclaimed Theatr Clwyd, Mold has a long history from the earliest times. It was a fixed settlement of the Normans, who built a motte and bailey castle on Bailey Hill. Being a border town, it changed hands between the Normans and the Welsh several times, and both lead- and coal-mining were important local industries. On 7 July 1990 we see two Reebur-bodied Mercedes-Benz 709D mini-buses, MMM 377 (G177 FJC) to the right, working on Service B4, and to the left the rear of MMM 372 (G172 FJC), both new to Crosville Cymru in 1989. In the background can be seen the Parish Church of St Mary's in Wales.

On 10 November 2004, with few leaves left on the trees, there is a clearer view of the church and its surroundings. The bus station has undergone some changes as we see Arriva Dennis Dart/Plaxton Pointer 2328 (S848 RJC) showing Route X44 heading for Chester. *John Robinson/JCH*

MOLD, PONTERWYL DEPOT: New in about 1923/24, the depot was enlarged in 1937. In 1947 it had an allocation of 42, 39 in 1956, 38 in 1965, and 32 in 1970. It continued in use with Crosville Cymru until October 1999 when the new depot at Manor Lane, Hawarden, was opened. In our 'past' photo, dated about 1985, a Bristol VR advertising Leo's at Saltney is about to leave the depot.

The depot was subsequently demolished in December 1999, and the site sold for re-development, but none had occurred by 10 November 2004, when GHA Coaches' all-Leyland Olympian G309 UYK passed by. The bus was new in London, then went to UK North of Gorton prior to GHA. Only the brick gateposts remain to 'lock' the photos together. *Both JCH*

NEFYN is situated on the north coast of the Lleyn peninsula, close to neighbouring Morfa Nefyn with its excellent sandy beach. On 10 March 1986 Bristol VR DVG 530 (DCA 530X) heads for Pwllheli on Route 8, with a background of glorious countryside.

Nearly 20 years later, on 24 March 2005, the route number remains the same as Nefyn Coaches' Mercedes-Benz N514 FJC climbs the hill out of the village en route to Pwllheli. There has been some tree growth but the view is otherwise unchanged. *Chris Lodington/JCH*

PENMAENMAWR: On 28 June 1976 Bristol FS DFG 222 (JFM 222D) passes through the town working on Route M5 between Llandudno and Caernarfon.

The route number 5 is still the same for Arriva's service between the towns, although the 5X runs only as far as Bangor. On 22 February 2005 Arriva Dennis Dart/Alexander 2279 (P961 RUL) is en route to Caernarfon. On the left-hand side the verandah has gone, as has the conical tower just beyond. Note the snow on the hillside. *Chris Lodington/JCH*

PORTHMADOG is a busy town and holiday resort at the north-east corner of Cardigan Bay, once an extremely active port exporting slate and home of two narrow-gauge railways (the Ffestiniog and the Welsh Highland). On 13 August 1968 Bristol MW SMG 391 (848 RFM) is seen leaving southwards, passing Britannia Terrace, on Service R28 from Llanfrothen. Note the 'old' spelling of 'Portmadoc'. A well-known bus stop in the main street is known as 'Australia', referring to a nearby public house!

The terrace appears to be little changed in the second picture of Express Motors' Mercedes-Benz WDZ 4138, while a few hundred yards back into the town the third picture shows the sign of the above-mentioned 'Australia' pub, with Arriva DAF/Van Hool 5003 (M945 LYR) on Route X32 to Aberystwyth; both photographs were taken on 15 February 2005. The latter vehicle is in branded livery for Route 701, which at the time ran between Aberystwyth and Cardiff/Porth. New to Grey Green, the bus was one of a pair that came to Arriva Cymru to originally work the Traws Cambria service. For February it was a bright sunny day and the town was remarkably full of people (and cars). *Chris Lodington/JCH (2)*

PRESTATYN is the first of the popular holiday resorts along the North Wales coast as one travels from the east. Open-top Bristol FSF DFG 81 (891 VFM) approaches the railway bridge from Talacre on Service M87 in August 1982. It is passing ex-Merseyside PTE 1134 (UKA 585H), a 'Jumbo' Leyland Atlantean/Alexander of Les Hughes, Rhyl, on a competing service.

Just over 22 years later, on 10 November 2004, the Royal Victoria remains unchanged as Arriva Dennis Dart/Plaxton Pointer 843 (Y543 UJC) climbs the hill working on Route 35, which is a Rhyl circular via Prestatyn and Rhuddlan. *A. Moyes/JCH*

PWLLHELI is the principal town and holiday resort on the southern shore of the Lleyn peninsula, its Wednesday market being one of the busiest in the UK, while its new marina has berths for more than 400 boats. Low-floor Dennis Dart/Plaxton Pointer LDC 521 (R521 UCC) pauses at the setting-down stop on 10 October 1997. This special livery commemorated the partnership between Crosville Cymru and Gwynedd County Council.

The scene was much the same when photographed on 24 March 2005. Arriva Dennis Dart/Plaxton Pointer 1130 (N707 GUM) has set down its passengers working on Route 17B from Aberdaron. Behind is similar bus 821 (W269 NFF) arriving on Route 3 from Porthmadog. *Both JCH*

RHYL/Y RHYL is another popular resort on the North Wales coast with a long sea-front. Its mini 'Golden Mile' has all the usual amusements with wonderful views from the 240-foot Skytower on the Promenade. On 14 September 1985 we see Northern Counties-bodied Daimler Fleetline HDG 903 (TCD 373J), bought second-hand in 1980 from Southdown and converted to open-top by Crosville in 1984 for use at Rhyl. It is named *Castell Caernarfon* and is seen at the bus station, employed on route M82. It was later to be transferred to Crosville Cymru on 10 August 1986.

In the 'present' photo taken on 25 June 2004 we see that the Astra cinema/bingo hall has been re-named Apollo. Buses now use the area immediately in front of the railway station, and awaiting departure is Arriva Mercedes-Benz/Plaxton Beaver 343 (R113 TKO). Behind is Dennis Dart/Plaxton Pointer 1325 (P825 RWU) on Route 11, which runs between Chester and Rhyl. *John Robinson/JCH*

RHYL: In May 1952 ECOC-bodied Leyland Tiger TS7 KA 7 (FM 9971) stands at the bus station in front of the railway station, waiting its next turn of duty on Route 420 to Trelogan. This bus was new to Crosville in 1936, so had already put in 16 years of service.

Moving on 52 years to 10 November 2004, while the bus station has been re-modelled there is little major change. The station buildings are much the same, although having undergone considerable refurbishment. Arriva Dennis Dart/Plaxton Pointer 2350 (V580 DJC) is working on Route 12 to Llandudno, with two Arriva Mercedes-Benz minibuses to the left. *Both JCH*

The third photograph, dated 14 September 1985, shows the old bus station building that was in use in the town centre. Operated on a one-way system, Leyland National SNL 883 (RFM 883M) is about to leave on Route M83 to Llys Brenig. The bus was new to Crosville in 1974, and following the break-up of the company went to Bee Line in 1989. The bus station closed in 1990. *John Robinson*

RHYL DEPOT: Opened in 1930, Fynnongroew Road Depot had an allocation of 55 vehicles in 1947, reducing slightly to 51 in 1980. In the picture of 2 October 1983, taken from the nearby railway footbridge, Leyland National SNL 560 (HMA 560T) is visible.

Twenty-one years later, on 25 June 2004, apart from the change of name to Arriva, there has been little alteration, apart from the re-roofing of the building in the foreground and the disappearance of the storage tank in the background. The lower half of ex-Merseybus open-top Leyland Olympian/Alexander 3984 (E224 WBG) can be seen just below the depot roof. *Both JCH*

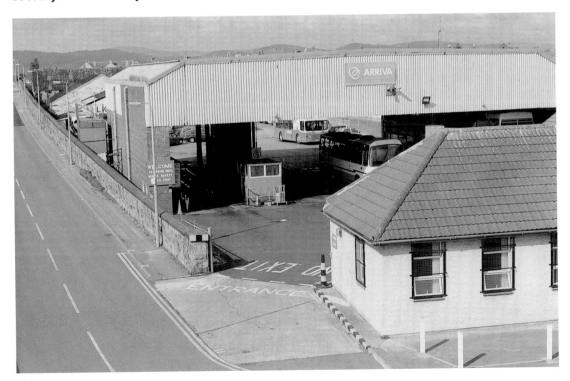

RUTHIN/RHUTHUN is the market town centre of the Vale of Clwyd, and is famous for the various periods of its architecture. The castle, which dated from the time of Edward I on what is believed to be a medieval site, has been converted into an hotel. Bristol VR DVL 444 (RMA 444V) picks up passengers outside the Council Offices on 27 February 1993, employed on Service B5 to Mold.

GHA Coaches' Mercedes-Benz/Plaxton Beaver P225 LKK is working the same Route 5 on 15 February 2005, having arrived at Market Street from Mold, and will shortly operate the return service. A new building has appeared on the right-hand side and the Council Offices are now a 'One Stop' retail outlet. There is a light scattering of snow on the hills in the background. *Chris Lodington/JCH*

TAN-Y-BWLCH: On 11 August 1984 Bristol RE ERG 277 (YFM 277L) is outside the Oakeley Arms on Service R3 from Pwllheli to Blaenau Ffestiniog. Strategically placed between Porthmadog and Blaenau Ffestiniog, where several main roads meet, this is an excellent place for an Interchange (there is also a railway station nearby on the Ffestiniog Railway).

On 9 March 2005 Express Motors Optare Spectra EM04 ORS passes the Oakeley Arms en route to Blaenau Ffestiniog. *John Young/JCH*

Gwynedd Council built a very attractive bus shelter here, which won an award for design using local materials. The Tany-y-Bwlch Interchange offers real-time information for the traveller. *JCH*

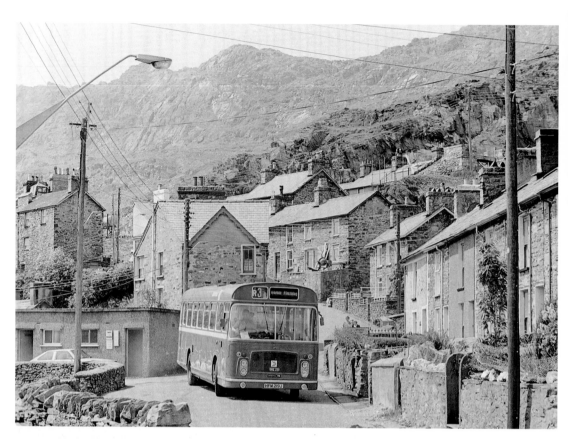

TAN-Y-GRISIAU: Only a mile or so from Blaenau Ffestiniog, this small village is set in the heart of the slate country. In this atmospheric picture of 21 June 1983, Bristol RE SRG 219 (HFM 219J) is seen working Service R3 by Dolydd Terrace. At the time this local service went through from Blaenau Ffestiniog to Pwllheli. The houses are dwarfed by the mountains behind.

The view of 9 March 2005 remains much the same. John's Coaches' 'Clipa'-branded Mercedes-Benz/Plaxton Beaver N671 TPF has just turned and is heading back to Blaenau Ffestiniog on the local Route 37. *A. Moyes/JCH*

Anglesey/Ynys Môn

ABERFFRAW was the ancient seat of the powerful Princes of Gwynedd. On 4 September 1975 Bristol RE SRG 119 (AFM 119G) approaches the village with a Bangor-Newborough-Llangefni N42 service. The mountains of Snowdonia on the mainland can be seen in the background.

On 2 March 2005, other than some changes to the bridge structure, the view is unaltered, although the distant mountains are shrouded in low cloud. Arriva Dennis Dart/East Lancs 1308 (N528 SPA) is also heading for Llangefni on Route 42 from Bangor. *A. Moyes/JCH*

AMLWCH was once close to the world's largest source of copper – Parys Mountain – which brought prosperity to the port. Crosville opened Lon Goch depot in 1935; it usually had an allocation of a dozen buses between 1947 and 1965, but by 1970 it had dropped to six, and the garage was reduced to outstation status by 1968. In this view, taken on 28 November 1982, a Plaxton-bodied Bristol RE coach is parked outside.

The depot remained open under Crosville Cymru until October 1990, when agreement was made with Lewis y Llan to house the vehicles and the original site was re-developed as a Kwik Save supermarket in 1992. Visited on 2 March 2005, the houses at the rear and to the right are the link between 'past' and 'present'. Lewis y Llan-operated Dennis Dart/Plaxton S4 SYA approaches the terminus (referred to as 'Kwiks' in the Anglesey timetable) working Route 61 from Holyhead. *Both JCH*

BEAUMARIS/BIWMARES is the location of another of King Edward I's castles (claimed to be the perfect concentric castle) and the last of the 'ring' around North Wales – in fact it was never completed, but is nonetheless of great interest. Now a popular holiday resort, the town is said to have an 'English feel', which no doubt dates back to when the local people were evicted and it became a garrison town. In July 1956 brand-new Bristol LS UG 337 (486 AFM) heads for Bangor on Service 516.

Nearly 50 years later, on 2 March 2005, Arriva Mercedes-Benz/Alexander 393 (W193 CDN) is about to depart for Bangor on Route 57. The castle walls can be seen in the background, but apart from some changes of ownership the buildings appear much the same. *John Fozard/JCH*

HOLYHEAD/CAERGYBI is the prime port in Wales for ferries to Ireland, carrying passengers, vehicles and freight. Hundreds of thousands of people pass through each year, perhaps not realising how close they are to the wonderfully spectacular scenery of the coast by South Stack lighthouse. On 2 July 1983 ex-Eastern National Bristol VR DVG 553 (SMS 32H) passes along Victoria Road by the docks, with one of the Irish ferry ships in the background. The bus shows 'Rio Tinto' on the blind, referring to Rio Tinto Zinc, the manufacturers of aluminium (now Anglesey Aluminium), whose factory is not far out of the town.

Twenty-odd years later, on 13 January 2005, following the 'arrival' of the new A55 in the town, there have been many changes. The wall by the railway has gone, although the building behind remains. Arriva VDL/Wrightbus Cadet 2481 (CX04 AXY) has just picked up passengers as it works Route 4 to Bangor. *Both JCH*

HOLYHEAD, RHOS-Y-GAER DEPOT: Opened in 1930 following the purchase of Holyhead Motors (Mona Maroon), between 1947 and 1970 the allocation varied between 9 and 14 buses, and for years the telephone number was Holyhead 2! On 2 July 1983 we see Bristol MW recovery vehicle G410 (430 UFM), and Bristol RE ERG 272 (YFM 272L) awaiting its next turn of duty.

The 'present' picture was taken on 13 January 2005, and while the depot building remains the same, it is now used by 'Wheels Self Drive'. *Both JCH*

Below The view looking down on the garage in October 1983 was taken from the deck of an Irish ferry! A Bristol VR and four REs can be seen outside the new building. *A. Moyes*

LLANERCHYMEDD is in the north of the island, famous for having produced snuff and boots – it is said that well over 250 cobblers worked here in 1833! Nearly 150 years later, in March 1975, Bristol MW EMG 347 (237 FFM) passes on Service N5 to Amlwch.

There have been a number of changes in the village, but using the mini-roundabout as a link, Arriva Dennis Dart/Plaxton Pointer 821 (W269 NFF) has come in on Route 63 from Bangor and turned round to start its return journey on 2 March 2005. *John Robinson/JCH*

LLANGEFNI DEPOT: Llangefni is the county town of Anglesey; situated in a central position on the island, it is a busy market town and nearby Oriel Ynys Môn is an important centre for the Arts. The depot was situated on Bridge Street, having been opened by Crosville in 1930 with the acquisition of UNU, and usually had an allocation of 7-9 vehicles. In the photo of 18 June 1983 the garage contains several buses including Leyland Nationals SNL 653 (GMB 653T) and SNL 570 (HMA 570T). Closed in 1986/7 and transferred to NBC Estates Ltd for subsequent sale, it was recorded as being open in 1988 under Crosville Cymru.

The building remains in situ on 2 March 2005 – there have been a few minor changes to the front but otherwise it is little different, although it does not appear to be in current use. *Both JCH*

MENAI BRIDGE/PORTHAETHWY is named after the famous Thomas Telford suspension bridge across the nearby Strait, wonderful views of which can be enjoyed from Belgian Promenade. Passing through the town in July 1956, Bristol Lodekka ML 665 (RFM 410), new two years earlier, is en route to Bangor, having come via Benllech. Note the local operator's Bedford OB coach on the right with the board advertising coach tours.

Although the location was easy to find, few buses approach the junction today. Arriva Dennis Dart/East Lancs 1304 (M524 MPF) is on its way to Beaumaris on Service 53 from Bangor Clock on 2 March 2005; surprisingly, it turned right and was not seen again! *John Fozard/JCH*

Mid and South West Wales

ABERAERON is a delightful seaside town on Cardigan Bay, mainly Georgian in character, with many of the buildings painted in attractive colours. On 8 May 1986, south-west of the town, Bristol RE ERG 270 (YFM 270L) climbs the steep hill on Route S57 to Caerwedros.

In the 'present' picture of 13 April 2005, Arriva DAF/Northern Counties 1796 (N24 FWU) is working on Route 550 to Cardigan. The view over the town and beyond is now partially obscured by the line of small trees etc at the roadside. *A. Moyes/JCH*

ABERAERON, LOWER REGENT STREET DEPOT was officially opened in March 1949. There had been an earlier parking area in Market Street, but it was affected by flooding, being close to the river. In the 'past' photo, taken in 1987, Leyland National SNL 410 (LMA 410T) is on the left with a 'sister' vehicle in the garage. The allocation varied between four buses in 1947 and eight in 1970. It remained open under Crosville Cymru until closure in 1990.

The buildings were demolished in 1993 and the area is now a car park, but the fire station and other nearby buildings tie the two pictures together, as seen on 13 April 2005. *A. Moyes/JCH*

ABERYSTWYTH is the largest resort on the west coast, home to the University College of Wales and the National Library of Wales. The ruins of one of the first castles built by Edward I are on the seafront, although on a much smaller scale than Caernarfon or Conwy. Captured by Owain Glyndwr in 1404, it was re-taken four years later. The ever-popular Vale of Rheidol narrow-gauge railway (to Devil's Bridge) shares the station with the standard gauge line. In British Rail days, Bristol RE SRG 93 (XFM 93G), on Route S14 to Machynlleth, is seen in front of the attractive façade of the railway station in March 1973.

Since then a new one-way system has been introduced, so that no vehicles pass the same way as the bus is facing; in addition, a new bus station has been built close to the station, to the left off camera, making comparisons difficult. On 21 September 2004 continuous traffic also made taking photographs difficult. The town is very much dominated by Arriva, but here we see Brodyr James Dennis Javelin/Plaxton Paramount 329 UWL is about to terminate. The front of the railway station has been converted to an eating place by J. D. Wetherspoon and the building carries the title of Yr Hen Orsaf – The Old Station. *A. Moyes/JCH*

ABERYSTWYTH DEPOT at Park Avenue was opened in 1934; its allocation in 1947 was 28, reducing to 21 in 1980. This rear view of the depot on 20 January 1998, when owned by Crosville Cymru, shows several Bristol VRs present.

In 2001 the depot became part of the Arriva Group with an allocation of 37 vehicles, having outstations at Abermule, Llanrhystud, New Quay and Tregaron. The depot suffered considerable damage in the winter gales of 2000 and was subsequently rebuilt on the same site, as seen in our 'present' photograph taken on 21 September 2004. From left to right are ERF recovery vehicle DSO 309T, a Leyland Lynx, Leyland Olympian and a line-up of mainly Alexander (Belfast)-bodied Volvo school buses in yellow, but next to the nearest is a Leyland Tiger/Alexander. *Both JCH*

BORTH is a small resort where a shingle bank separates the low-lying village from extensive sands. It was in the county of Dyfed, now Caredigion, and has a railway station on the Cambrian Line dating back to 1863. On 1 March 1986 Bristol VR DVG 568 (HAL 105K), new to East Midland, pulls up the hill at Upper Borth to Heol Aberwennol on a lunchtime Aberystwyth-Ynylas service, showing Service S12 'Ynyslas Turn' on the blinds.

Nineteen years later, on 16 April 2005, a lick of paint has brightened the scene and the bus approaching is Arriva Dennis Dart/Plaxton Pointer 1326 (P826 RWU). A few hundred yards further on it will turn and return en route to Aberystwyth via Bow Street on Route 512. *A. Moyes/JCH*

CARDIGAN/ABERTEIFI is a pleasant town on the River Teifi, with the remains of a castle that was reputedly the site of the first Eisteddfod in 1176. It is a meeting place also for buses, as in the photo of 17 September 1993, with Crosville Cymru (ex-Stevensons and Midland Fox) Bristol VR EVG 50 (PFA 50W) picking up passengers for its return to Aberystwyth on Route 550. On the right is Bedford YRT/Duple Dominant JKO 64N of Brodyr Richards (new in 1975 to Maidstone Borough Council), working to Haverfordwest, and to the left is the front end of a Rees of Crymach single-decker.

While Arriva, First and Mid Wales Motors are all to be seen in the town, it is Richard Bros that dominates the area today. On 14 April 2005, with St Mary's Church of Wales in the background, we see two of that company's buses, both showing Route X50, 'Aberystwyth trwy (via) Aberaeron'. Nearest the camera is Transbus Enviro SN53 KKZ, and behind it is Dennis Dart/Plaxton Pointer M740 DDE. *John Young/JCH*

LAMPETER/LLANBEDR PONT STEFFAN is a university and market town situated in the upper Vale of Teifi. It developed from a ford across the river, and is situated some 13 miles or so inland from Aberaeron. On 4 July 1975 Bristol RE ERG 285 (YFM 285L) pauses in the High Street on the morning Aberystwyth to Ammanford journey. The Town Hall/Courtroom building on the right is of considerable historical and architectural value.

Twenty-five years later the scene has changed very little although today only the first floor of the Town Hall is used for Town Council meetings. On 9 April 2005 Arriva Dennis Dart/Plaxton Pointer 1129 (N704 GUM) has just pulled in from Aberystwyth, working on Route X40 to Carmarthen. *A. Moyes/JCH*

LLANDYSUL/LLANDYSSIL is situated by the River Teifi in the heart of what was once a woollen producing area; its history stretches beyond Roman times to the earlier Iron Age. Dual-purpose Bristol REs (ERGs) were dominant at Crosville's ex-Western Welsh depot at Newcastle Emlyn in the 1980s, and ERG 279 (YFM 279L) is seen on the Capel Iwan school contract Route S50 (picked up from Western Welsh in 1972 and held until 1990) passing along New Road in the town on 1 July 1986.

On 11 April 2005 First Coaches Dennis Javelin/Plaxton Expressliner 21098 (R298 AYB) has dropped off a number of students. The road and area around the bus station have been modernised and the building behind the bus has gained a roof-mounted clock. In the background is the Parish Church of St Tysul. In the road improvement the 'hill' has been smoothed out a little! *A. Moyes/JCH*

MACHYNLLETH: A Charter was granted in 1291 by Edward I who gave the Lord of Powys the right to hold a market every Wednesday and two fairs every year in perpetuity. The town's greatest claim to fame, however, is its connection with Owain Glyndwr, who was crowned Prince of Wales here in 1404 and held his parliament in the town. In 1969 Bristol SC SSG 609 (342 CFM) pulls out on the Wednesday Service S20 to Talywern, with the attractive Memorial Clock in the background, erected by the townspeople in 1874 to celebrate the 21st birthday of Charles, Viscount Castlereagh. The vehicle was originally fleet number SC9 and fitted from new in 1957 for one-man operation.

The amount of traffic on 21 September 2004 was very different, with cars, vans and lorries parked on both sides of the road. Lloyds Coaches' Mercedes-Benz/Alexander P387 FEA approaches on local Service 34. *A. Moyes/JCH*

MACHYNLLETH, HEOL DOLL (DOLL STREET) DEPOT: Built and opened in the mid-1930s, it had an allocation of eight buses in 1947, remaining much the same until 1980, when there were seven. On 15 June 1985 Bristol VR DVG 573 (NCK 983K), bought from Ribble in 1983, stands outside the depot showing Service S18 'Dinas Mawddwy' on the blind. In the depot is a coach branded 'Traws Cambria'.

On 21 September 2004 there have been detail changes to the building, and Lloyds Coaches Mercedes-Benz/Alexander P387 FEA stands outside, with Service 34 indicated. Having been used by Crosville Cymru, after a period of being empty the garage was taken back into use by Arriva, who upgraded the building in 1999, including the provision of an inside lavatory for the first time! By 2004 it had outstation status, but from 5 June of that year was vacated by Arriva and is now in use by Wyn Lloyd's fleet. Arriva buses are now parked by the railway station, with fuelling taking place at Aberystwyth, Dolgellau and Abermule. *Both JCH*

NEWCASTLE EMLYN/CASTELL NEWYDD EMLYN DEPOT: This is a busy market town situated in the Teifi Valley offering good shopping and welcoming inns. The name relates to a 'new' castle built by the Welsh in a loop of the river in about 1240, now a ruin, having been blown up during the Civil War. A centre of Nonconformism in the 19th century, it has an impressive Bethel chapel. In 1972 Crosville took over the garage of Western Welsh, and in the first photo we see ex-Western Welsh Weymann-bodied Leyland Tiger Cub STL 930 (MUH 146) and indigenous Bristol SC SSG 602 (335 CFM) side-by-side.

Crosville Cymru continued to use the depot, as seen in the second picture, until the lease ran out in 1990, and it closed the same year following the loss of services to Davies Pencader.

Visited on 11 April 2005, the depot building remains intact but seemingly not in use. Richards Bros LDV Convoy BX54 FRF is seen passing the garage as it leaves the town. *A. Moyes (2)/JCH*

NEW QUAY/CEI NEWYDD DEPOT: New Quay is a popular holiday destination, situated at the southern end of Cardigan Bay, with a picturesque stone quay that, together with the beach, is sheltered by the nearby headland. It is claimed to be the 'Llareggub' of Dylan Thomas's *Under Milk Wood*. The original depot was built by Western Welsh in 1936 and the 'past' picture was taken a fortnight before it passed to Crosville in April 1972. Park Royal-bodied Leyland Tiger Cub DBO 353C (later to be designated STL 936) is in the entrance.

The depot building remains intact, as seen on 13 April 2005, although now part of a discount clothing shop. *A. Moyes/JCH*

At the rear of the garage on the same day in 1972, the Metro-Cammell-bodied Leyland Tiger Cub that would become STL 933 (UKG 274) is on the parking ground-cum-bus station.

Today the scene is little changed. On the right is Arriva Dennis Dart/Plaxton Pointer 832 (X272 RFF), awaiting departure to Cardigan on Route 550. *A. Moyes/JCH*

WELSHPOOL/Y TRALLWNG is a busy border town close to Powis Castle, with its origins dating back to about 1200. It is home to the Welshpool & Llanfair Light Railway, which runs for 8 miles to Llanfair Caereinion, and also has a Network Rail station on the route from Shrewsbury to Aberystwyth/Pwllheli. In October 1987 we see three Crosville Cymru vehicles outstationed at Welshpool, all displaying blinds for the Shrewsbury-Llanidloes service: Leyland National ENL 842 (NFM 840M) is sandwiched between two Bristol REs, ERG 283 (YFM 283L) and SRG 208 (HFM 208J).

The area has been subsequently converted to a large modern car park, but coaches/buses still use the far side by the Shropshire Union Canal for parking. On 9 April 2005 the front end of Worthen Travel DAF MB200/Jonckheere Bermuda XRP 757W is in the designated area. Across the car park can be seen the Church of St Mary of the Salutation, which links the two photographs together. *A. Moyes/JCH*

Index of locations

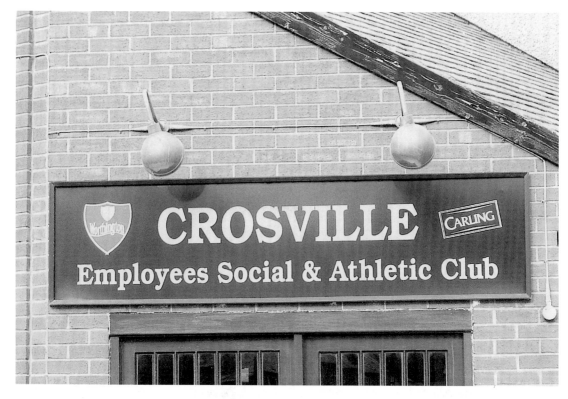

The name lingers on: this picture was taken in Bangor, opposite the old Crosville depot, on 22 February 2005. *JCH*